OVERCOMING OBSTACLES
in **COOKING**

MATTHEW W. MILLER

Copyright © 2022 Matthew W. Miller

All rights reserved. No part of this book may be reproduced, stored, or transmitted by any means—whether auditory, graphic, mechanical, or electronic—without written permission of both publisher and author, except in the case of brief excerpts used in critical articles and reviews. Unauthorized reproduction of any part of this work is illegal and is punishable by law.

ISBN: 978-1-957203-77-5 (sc)
ISBN: 978-1-957203-78-2 (hc)
ISBN: 978-1-957203-79-9 (e)

Because of the dynamic nature of the Internet, any web addresses or links contained in this book may have changed since publication and may no longer be valid. The views expressed in this work are solely those of the author and do not necessarily reflect the views of the publisher, and the publisher hereby disclaims any responsibility for them.

The Ewings Publishing LLC
One Galleria Blvd., Suite 1900, Metairie, LA 70001
1-888-421-2397

To my parents the late Donna G. and Wayne O. Miller who helped me overcome many obstacles.

ACKNOWLEDGEMENTS

I would like to thank my publisher, Marcus Lane and the staff at The Ewings Publishing for your help and support. I would also like to thank the following family members for providing delicious recipes; Bill and the late Eloise Smith, the late Dolores Helms, David and Linda Johnston, Cheryle Johnston Capps, Sandra Halterman, Janice Gerth, Christa Halterman Conner, Kay Smith, and Kelli Smith von Arnswaldt. I would also like to thank my friends Jerry Thomas and Autumn Smith for submitting their recipes. Thank you Jewell Devall for letting me use your kitchen to cook. Thank you Brad Wilks for helping me cook the recipes.

INTRODUCTION

I wrote this book to help those who want to overcome their addictions. I want it be used in mental hospitals, Liberty University's Global Center for Addiction and Recovery. Liberty University hire people with disabilities sooner because they may be going through domestic abuse. Pay your employees more so they can live on their own. Help people get traditional book deals sooner so they don't have to go through abuse. I also hope that it will be used in prison ministry programs. I hope this book will be used to help those going through domestic abuse. I hope churches well use this book to help prison inmates.

I am going to a mental hospital for the rest of my life in 2022. I have overcome a series of addictions. My addictions started with overeating food, then it continued with looking at porn. My dad was physically and mentally abusive to me and my brothers. In the mid-1990s, two of my brothers and I tried sex for the first time. We did this to deal with dad physically and mentally abusing us. I continued looking at porn in high school.

In 2000 I started community college. I looked at porn while I was a work study. I did this because my family and I were still being abused by my dad. In 2002 I moved to Lynchburg, VA. I started college at Liberty University because I wanted to get away from the domestic abuse that I was going though. Thank you to all who were kind to me at Liberty. I had an inappropriate conversation in the computer lab. My account was blocked for a while and I had to go to counseling and Bible study. While in college I had sex with men because I didn't believe in myself. I believed God did not help those with disabilities. I wanted a wife but some women expect a man to be totally perfect before they will help them.

In 2007 I moved back to Lynchburg because I didn't want to go through abuse in Culpeper. I continued to hurt myself because I was trying to work 2 jobs at one time to support myself. I worked retail overnight and subbed during the day. I took the jobs because I was going through domestic abuse. I tried to get a job at a college but didn't have paid experience Employees will never get paid experience unless you hire them.

In 2009 I moved back to Culpeper. One of my sister-in laws promised to go with me to a vocational counselor. She did not. My roomate tried to help me but was stressed out from work. He would not let me clean or practice safety procedures. I tried to hurt myself by eating outdated food and drinking chemicals. I did this because people would not clean up after themselves in a store. Also do not damage items like a Bible or writing pens. I ask for forgiveness for any pain I have caused. Be kind to everyone. I hope this book will be used to offer hope to those going through addiction. Matthew W. Miller.

MAIN DISHES

QUICK AND EASY BANANA SMOOTHIE

2 bananas
2 cups 1% milk
3 packets of Splenda or Splenda brown sugar mix

Cut the bananas into small pieces. Put the bananas into blender and add milk. Open packets of Splenda and pour into the blender. If you want brown sugar in the smoothie use Splenda brown sugar mix in place of just Splenda. Blend on high for 2-3 minutes and then pour into glasses and serve.

Good breakfast or snack for people with diabetes.

Submitted by: Matthew Miller

Tip: Peeling bananas helps strengthen fine motor skills.

EPHESIANS 5:9: For the fruit of the Spirit *is* in all goodness and righteousness and truth.

MUSHROOM MEAT PUFFS

1 onion, chopped
1 ½ cup soft bread crumbs
1 ½ teaspoon salt
1 can cream of mushroom soup
1 ½ pounds ground beef
2 eggs
¼ teaspoon Worcestershire sauce
1 ½ soup cans water

Mix onion, ground beef, bread crumbs eggs, salt and Worcestershire sauce. Shape into balls. Brown in skillet; drain. Put meatballs back into skillet before combining soup with water. Cover and simmer 30-40 minutes. Cook until soup is thickened.

Submitted by: Donna Miller

My mom loved to sew and paint.

Poem I wrote in memory of her:

Mom's Crafts

Mom's crafts helped people
Big beautiful quilts, pot holders, and pillows
Torn scraps made into something useful
Boxes piled high, packed into the truck, and sent to the craft shop.
Mom's crafts made sure adults stayed warm.

PROVERBS 31:13: She seeketh wool, and flax, and worketh willingly with her hands.

CHICKEN CACCIATORE

1 whole chicken cut into pieces or 2-3 pounds chicken
2 cloves garlic, minced
1 8 oz. can mushroom pieces
1 bay leaf
¼ teaspoon allspice
2 cups hot water
1 onion, chopped
1 green pepper, chopped
1 8 oz. can tomato paste
½ teaspoon pepper
1 teaspoon salt

In a large skillet, brown the chicken in oil; add onion, garlic, green pepper, and mushrooms. Cook, stirring 4-5 minutes. Mix the tomato paste with the remaining ingredients and pour over chicken. Cover and simmer for 30 minutes, and then uncover and simmer until the sauce has reached the desired thickness. Transfer chicken to a casserole dish. Skim the fat from the sauce and pour it over chicken.

This is great served over rice!
Submitted by: Donna Miller

Tip: People with Cerebral Palsy may need more time to cook than people without this condition. Please be patient with them!

PROVERBS 31:15: She riseth also while it is yet night, and giveth meat to her household, and a portion to her maidens.

FAMILY-SIZE MEATLOAF

1 lb. ground beef
1 onion
1 teaspoon salt
1 tablespoon parsley flakes
½ cup ketchup
2 slices of bread, crumbled, or ½ cup of oatmeal
1 egg
½ teaspoon pepper
1 teaspoon Worcestershire sauce

Preheat oven to 400 degrees. Mix together all ingredients in a bowl. Pour into 8 by 8 in. baking dish and shape into a loaf. Bake for 1 hour. Add gravy if desired.

Gravy:

1 can cream of mushroom soup
1 teaspoon gravy maker
½ can water

Blend well and pour over the top of the shaped meatloaf just before serving.

I use this each time I make meatloaf, and it always turns out very tasty. It is easily doubled or tripled, but the standard measurements serve about 4 people.

Submitted by: Sandra Halterman

Tip: Do not shout or yell at someone with Cerebral Palsy if they do not learn something the first time. It may bring on their tremors.

MATTHEW 18:33: Shouldest not thou also have compassion on thy fellow servant, even as I had pity on thee?

KELLI'S FAVORITE OATMEAL WAFFLES

1 cup uncooked whole-grain oats (not instant)
1 cup fat-free cottage cheese
¼ teaspoon ground cinnamon
½ cup maple syrup (regular or sugar-free).

6 egg whites

¼ teaspoon vanilla extract
2 packets Splenda
¼ cup mixed berries (optional)

Lightly coat a waffle iron with cooking spray and turn the heat to medium. In a blender, combine oats, egg whites, cottage cheese, vanilla, cinnamon, and Splenda. Blend on medium speed until smooth, about 1 minute. Pour batter into the hot waffle maker. Cook until waffle iron stops steaming. While waffles are cooking, microwave the syrup until warm, about 20 seconds. Put syrup and berries on waffles if you like.

Submitted by: Kelli van Arnswaldt

Tip: People with learning disabilities may find it easier to concentrate in a quiet kitchen.

MATTHEW 13:29: But he said, Nay; lest while ye gather up the tares, ye root up also the wheat with them.

MANICOTTI MINER'S DELIGHT

9 eggs
1 ½ cup all-purpose flour
2 garlic cloves, minced
½ pound chopped mushrooms
1 ½ cups mozzarella cheese
¼ teaspoon oregano
3 teaspoons salt
½ cup grated Romano cheese
1 cup milk
2 cups onion, chopped
1 tablespoon olive oil
1 ½ pounds ground beef
1 cup soft bread crumbs
½ teaspoon pepper
1 ½ cups cottage cheese or ricotta
¼ cup chopped parsley
One 26-ounce jar of spaghetti sauce with mushrooms

Pancakes

Beat together 6 eggs, milk, flour, and ½ teaspoon of salt until well mixed. Cook the pancakes on a moderately hot crape pan on one side only. Makes 16 pancakes.

Meat Filling

Cook onion and garlic in the olive oil. Toss in the mushrooms; remove from heat. Stir in the ground beef, mozzarella, bread crumbs, 1 egg, 1 ½ teaspoons salt, oregano, and ¼ teaspoon pepper.

Cheese Filling

Preheat oven to 350 degrees. Combine cottage or ricotta cheese, Romano cheese, parsley, 2 eggs, 1 teaspoon salt, and ¼ teaspoon pepper.

Spoon the meat filling onto 8 pancakes and the cheese filling on the remaining 8 pancakes. Roll and place seam side down on a greased 13 by 9 by 2 in. baking dish. Spoon spaghetti sauce over top of rolls, sprinkle with cheese. Bake for 30-40 minutes. Makes 8 servings.

Note: Egg whites can be used in place of half of the eggs if you are watching your cholesterol.

Submitted by: Donna Miller and Eloise Smith

BREADS

BROCCOLI BREAD

1 stick of butter, melted
Pinch of salt
1 onion, chopped
1 box Jiffy cornbread mix

4 eggs
6 oz. cottage cheese or sour cream
1 box (10 ounces) frozen broccoli, thawed

Grease a glass sheet cake dish with stick of melted better. In a bowl, beat the eggs, mix in salt, cottage cheese or sour cream, onion, and broccoli. Pour the excess butter out of the baking pan and into the mixture and stir until incorporated. Add the Jiffy mix and stir until blended. Pour the batter into the greased baking dish and bake for 25-30 minutes or until golden brown.

Submitted by: Sandra Halterman

Tip: People with disabilities may be able to move around easier when a store is less crowded.

ACTS 27:35: And when he had thus spoken, he took bread, and gave thanks to God in the presence of them all: and when he had broken it, he began to eat.

TURTLES

3 cups all-purpose flour
1 teaspoon salt
⅓ cup of oil or shortening
3 teaspoons baking powder
1 tablespoon sugar
1 ½ cups milk

Put all ingredients in a large bowl and mix until the dough becomes stiff, about the consistency of drop cookies. Add more milk if necessary. Pour a small amount of oil into a cast-iron over medium heat and drop in the dough by the spoonful, spreading out each drop into a biscuit. 3-4 inches across. Brown on one side, then turn and tap, and cook on the other side. When the dough sounds like a turtle shell tapped, the biscuits are done.

Tip: Good with jam or jelly!

MATTHEW 6:11: Give us this day our daily bread.

ZUCCHINI BREAD

3 cups flour
1 teaspoon salt
¾ teaspoon baking soda
1 cup chopped nuts
3 eggs
1 cup sugar
1 teaspoon cinnamon
2 cups shredded, unpeeled zucchini
1 cup raisins
1 cup oil

Preheat the oven to 350 degrees. In large bowl, stir together flour, sugar, salt, cinnamon, baking soda, zucchini, nuts, and raisins. In another bowl, beat the eggs and oil. Pour over the flour mixture and stir until moistened. Pour the batter into an oiled 9 by 5 by 3 inch loaf pan. Bake for 35 minutes or until a toothpick inserted into the center comes out clean. Cool in pan for 10 minutes, and then turn out on a wire rack until cooled all the way.

Submitted by: Janice Gretch

Tip: Self-Checkout registers may help people with disabilities in stores because they can talk and they can work at their own pace when purchasing items.

PROVERBS 28:19: He that tilleth his land should have plenty of bread:

VEGETABLES

CHERYLE'S VEGETABLE SALSA

1 each of green, red, yellow, and orange bell peppers
1 onion
4 celery stalks
Fresh cilantro
2-3 cloves garlic, minced Garlic salt to taste
Juice of 2 limes

1 cucumber

Handful of carrots
1 hot pepper (your choice)
2 14 ounce cans of diced tomatoes

Using a food processor, finely chop the bell peppers, cucumber, onion, carrots, celery, hot pepper, and cilantro. Add the tomatoes, garlic, garlic salt, and lime juice and mix. Serve with tortilla chips

Note: Fresh tomatoes are better! Use 4-5 standard tomatoes. I also use Mexican diced tomatoes for extra flavor.

Submitted by: Cheryle Johnston Capps

Tip: People with disabilities may find it easier to make recipes that they do not have to bake.

PSALM 23:1-2: The Lord is my shepherd; I shall not want. He maketh me to lie down in green pastures: he leadth me beside the still waters.

YELLOW SQUASH FRITTERS

1 ¼ cups self-rising flour
½ teaspoon salt
1 egg
3 cups coarsely grated yellow squash
1 tablespoon vegetable oil
½ teaspoon sugar
½ cup sour cream
Pepper to taste (optional)
½ onion, chopped

Combine the first 5 ingredients, stirring until smooth and adding pepper if desired. Stir in grated squash and chopped onion. Heat vegetable oil in large skillet. Drop squash mixture by tablespoons into hot oil and cook until golden brown, turning once. Drain on paper towels.

Submitted by: Dolores Helms

Tip: Give people with disabilities "wait time." This means that when you show adults with disabilities how to cook, don't rush in and yell at them if they don't understand the first time. As an adult, people would ask me where something was and then yell at me if I didn't immediately know where it was. Only rush to help them if there is an emergency.

GALATIONS 5:5: For we through the Spirit wait for the hope for the hope of righteousness by faith.

SCALLOPED TOMATOES

1 onion, chopped
1 ½ cups dry unseasoned bread, cut into cubes
5 cups canned tomatoes
½ teaspoon freshly ground pepper
4 tablespoons butter
½ cup tightly packed brown sugar
1 teaspoon salt

Preheat oven to 350 degrees. Grease a shallow casserole dish. Saute the onion in butter until soft but not brown. Add the bread and brown sugar, reduce the heat to low, and stir for 3-5 minutes. Stir in tomatoes, add salt and pepper, and then pour mixture into the casserole dish. Bake for 30-40 minutes, or until bubbly.

Submitted by: Dolores Helms

Tip: Use bigger supplies and a bigger work space when cooking. More space and bigger kitchen gadgets may make it easier for people with disabilities to cook.

ACTS 2:42: And the continued steadfastly in the apostles' doctrine and fellowship, and in breaking of bread, and in prayers.

SPINACH-BROCCOLI BAKE

1 10 oz. package frozen chopped spinach
1 can (10 ¾ oz.) cream of mushroom soup
1 egg
¼ teaspoon salt
2 cups frozen broccoli
½ cup mayonnaise
½ teaspoon pepper
¼ teaspoon garlic powder

Preheat oven to 350 degrees. Place frozen vegetables in water and boil for 3 minutes. Drain. In mixing bowl, combine the remaining ingredients. Add the spinach and broccoli and pour into a greased 2-quart casserole dish. Bake for 40 minutes or until firm.

Submitted by: Kelli von Arnswaldt

Tip: If you take classes in college take the fewest amount of credits required for full-time status. Take classes during the summer to finish sooner.

MATTHEW 15:37a: And they did all eat, and were filled...

SOUPS AND SALADS

CHERYLE'S STEAK SALAD

1-2 cups cooked steak 1 bag salad mix

2 cups pasta, cooked as directed and cooled

1 onion

Other salad fixings as desired (tomatoes, cucumbers, etc.)

If using leftover steak, just slice and set aside. Otherwise, slice the steak into strips and stir-fry in 1 tablespoon olive oil with minced garlic until done. Sprinkle with garlic salt if desired. Set aside and let cool. In large bowl combine, salad mix, onion, pasta, and other fixings. Use red wine-thyme vinaigrette if desired.

Submitted by: Cheryle Johnson Capps

Tip: Do not damage or steal items in a store. This may cause people with disabilities to have panic attacks. By damaging an item you are keeping retail employees from putting out new items.

PSALM 51:1: Create in me a clean heart O God; and renew a right spirit within me.

RED WINE-THYME VINAIGRETTE

½ cup olive oil
½ teaspoon salt
2 teaspoons thyme leaves (not ground)
4 tablespoons red wine vinegar
¼ teaspoon ground red pepper
½ teaspoon minced garlic

Shake or stir until mixed.

Tip: Use ¼ teaspoon garlic powder if you do not have minced garlic.

PSALMS 86:15: But thou, O Lord, *art* a God full of compassion, and gracious, longsuffering, and plenteous in mercy and truth.

VENISON VEGETABLE SOUP

The day before making the soup, cook 3-4 lbs. venison ham roast with 2 teaspoons salt and 3 bouillon cubes in a Crock-Pot on high for 4 hours or on low for 8 hours until the roast is tender. Remove and cool overnight. Strain the broth and set aside for the soup.

Cut the meat into pieces. Then add it to the Crock Pot with:

- 1 tablespoon sugar
- 1 15 oz. can corn
- 1 large onion
- 1 package frozen mixed vegetables
- 1 can tomatoes
- 3 tablespoons chopped garlic
- 2 or 3 large potatoes
- 1 cup frozen peas

Makes approximately 1 gallon.

Add water, sliced onion, garlic, salt, pepper, and Worcestershire sauce. Cover and simmer (don't boil) for 1 ½ hours or until onion is tender. Add vegetables except for tomatoes and cook for 20 minutes. Add tomatoes and cook 15 minutes longer or until 15 minutes longer or until meat and vegetables are done. To thicken the liquid, stir 2 tablespoons cornstarch into ½ cup water until smooth. Stir into the stew and cook for 5 minutes or until thickened.

Makes 6 to 8 servings

Submitted by Kay Smith

Tip: OT means Occupational Therapist. They help you with activities of daily living such as cooking or picking up a coin.

JUDE 22: And of some have compassion, making a difference.

TACO SALAD

Note: Save 1 tablespoon of taco seasoning for the salad dressing.

- 1 lb. ground beef
- 1 head chopped lettuce
- 1 large red onion, chopped
- 2 cups shredded cheddar cheese
- 1 package of taco seasoning
- One 16-ounce can red beans, rinsed
- 4 tomatoes, seeded and diced
- One 7-½ oz. bag tortilla chips

Dressing

- One 8 oz. bottle of Thousand Island dressing
- 1 tablespoon taco seasoning mix
- 2 tablespoons taco sauce

Cook ground beef with taco seasoning. Layer beef, lettuce, beans, onion, tomatoes, cheese, and chips. Serve with dressing.

Submitted by: Kay Smith

Tip: Use cooking funnels to pour liquids.

I JOHN 1:9: If we confess our sins, he is faithful and just to forgive us *our* sins, and to cleanse us from all unrighteousness

FRUIT CUP SALAD

2 cups sour cream
One 8-ounce can crushed pineapple
¼ cup chopped pecans
⅛ teaspoon salt
2 tablespoons lemon juice
1 diced banana
½ cup sugar
4 drop red food coloring (optional)

Blend all ingredients together. Place in shallow pan and freeze. Slice into individual squares. Enjoy!

Submitted by: Kelli von Arnswaldt

Tip: Skip lines when writing down a recipe. Use wide ruled paper.

GALATIONS 5:22: But the fruit of the Spirit is love, joy, peace, longsuffering, gentleness, goodness, faith.

BROCCOLI SALAD

1 head fresh broccoli cut into florets
Bacon bits Red onion, chopped

4 oz. shredded cheddar cheese

Mix all ingredients together. In a separate bowl, mix the ingredients for the 3-in-1 dressing, as listed below, pour over the salad mixture, and mix well.

3-in-1 Dressing

1 cup mayonnaise or Miracle Whip
2 tablespoons vinegar

½ cup sugar

Submitted by: Christa Conner

Tip: Make sure you do not damage items in the salad dressing isle.

EPHESIANS 1:7: In whom we have redemption through his blood, the forgiveness of sins, according to the riches of his grace.

DESSERTS

CHOCOLATE BUTTERSCOTCH PUDDING CAKE

1 box devil's food cake mix
1 12 oz. container whipped topping
1 bag chocolate chips Chocolate sprinkles
1 bag pecan halves and pieces (optional)

1 box butterscotch instant pudding
1 jar maraschino cherries

Preheat oven to 350 degrees. Prepare the cake following the directions on the box and pour the cake batter into 2 9-inch cake pans. Bake the cakes for 30-33 minutes. Let cakes cool for 10-15 minutes before taking them out of the pans. Make sure the cake is completely cool before frosting.

When the cake is cool, mix the box of butterscotch pudding according to the package directions. Spread the pudding on the first cake layer. Then, sprinkle with chocolate chips. Put the second cake layer on top of the first. Frost the top and the sides of the cake with whipped topping. Remove the stems from the maraschino cherries and place the cherries on the cake in a circle around the edge. Sprinkle the cake with chocolate sprinkles, chocolate chips, and pecans if desired. Add more pecan halves around the outside of the cake if desired.

This is one of my favorite birthday cakes!

Submitted by: Donna Miller and Matthew Miller

Tip: Use "people first" language. People first language puts the person before their disability. Instead of saying learning disabled adult, you say adult with a learning disability.

I THESSALONIANS 5: 14:
Now we exhort you, brothern warn them that are unruly, comfort the feebleminded, support the weak, be patient toward all *men*.

SOUR CREAM COCONUT POUND CAKE

- 1 box butter golden cake mix
- ⅔ cup sugar
- 1 8-ounce container of sour cream
- 1 6-ounce frozen coconut, thawed
- 1 teaspoon baking powder
- 4 eggs
- 1 cup oil
- 1 teaspoon coconut
- 2 teaspoons salt
- 1 ½ cups milk

Mix all ingredients together and bake at 350 degrees for 55-60 minutes. I always bake this cake in a Bundt cake pan.

Everyone loves this cake!

Submitted by: Christa Conner

Tip: When learning to cook, focus on what you like to cook, not what you can't. If you like to bake cakes then just bake cakes.

JOHN 16:33a: These things I have spoken to you, that in me, ye might have peace...

DONNA'S TOFFEE BUTTER COOKIES

1 cup butter
1 egg
2 cups flour
Eight 2 oz. plain milk chocolate bars or ½ pound chocolate chips
1 cup brown sugar
1 teaspoon vanilla
¼ cup nuts

Preheat oven to 350 degrees. Cream the butter and the sugar. Add the egg and beat until light and fluffy. Add the vanilla and flour and blend thoroughly. Spread the dough into an 11 by 7 in. pan and bake for 15-20 minutes. Place the chocolate bars or chocolate chips on top of the hot dough and allow to melt, and then spread the chocolate out. Sprinkle the chocolate with sprinkles and chopped nuts.

Donna, who gave Kay Smith this recipe was known for all the wonderful desserts she made. This recipe was no exception!

Submitted by: Kay Smith

Tip: Use an airtight container to store the leftover cookies in.

JOHN 14:6: Jesus saith unto him, I am the way, the truth, and the life: no man cometh unto the Father but by me.

FRUIT PIZZA COOKIES

1 package of sugar cookie dough
1 banana, sliced into thin discs
1 container of blueberries
8-ounce container of whipped topping
1 container of raspberries
1 container of strawberries

Bake the sugar cookie dough according to the package directions Let the cookies cool for 10-15 minutes on top of the stove. Transfer the cookies to a plate. Spread whipped topping on sugar cookie then top with fruit of your choice.

I adapted a fruit pizza recipe to fit on a sugar cookie.

Tip: Make sugar cookies from scratch using your recipe.

Submitted by: Matthew Miller

PHILIPPIANS 1:11: Being filled with the fruits of righteousness, which are by Jesus Christ, unto the glory and praise of God.

CUSTARD PIE

2 ½ cups milk
½ cup sugar
2 pinches, nutmeg

3 large eggs
1 teaspoon salt

Scald the milk and blend in the eggs, sugar, salt, and nutmeg. Pour into an unbaked pie shell. Sprinkle additional nutmeg on top. Bake at 400 degrees for 25-30 minutes.

Submitted by: Lottie Gutshall and Eloise Smith

Tip: Use prepared pie shells instead of having to make your own.

COLOSSIANS 3:17: And whatsoever ye do in word or deed, *do* all in the name of the Lord Jesus, giving thanks to God and the Father by him.

RECIPIES AND TIPS FROM FRIENDS

BROWN SUGAR PORK CHOPS

1 package of boneless center-cut pork chops

1 stick butter

Salt and pepper to taste

1 cup brown sugar

Preheat oven to 375 degrees. In a shallow glass baking dish, place the pork chops flat. Cut the butter into pats and lay them on top of each pork chop. Season with salt and pepper to taste. Cover each pork chop with a generous amount of brown sugar. Roast in the oven for 20 minutes. Flip the pork chops over and salt and pepper to taste. Add another generous amount of brown sugar on the other side. Replace in the oven and roast another 10 minutes. Check the internal temperature is 140 degrees with a meat thermometer. Remove from the oven, allow to cool and then serve.

Submitted by: Jerry Thomas, Jr.

Tip: Boneless pork chops are easier for people with disabilities to use because they do not have to pull out bones.

I TIMOTHY 6:8: And having food and raiment let us be therewith content.

WINTER BLACK BEAN SALSA

1 16-ounce can black beans, rinsed and drained
1 tomato, chopped
1 envelope of garlic and herb salad dressing mix
½ teaspoon fresh jalapeno pepper, minced
Tortilla chips

1 10-ounce bag of corn
¼ cup fresh lime juice
2 tablespoons cilantro, chopped
¼ teaspoon, ground cumin

Mix all ingredients in a large bowl until well blended; cover. Refrigerate 15 minutes. Serve with tortilla chips. Store leftovers in a container in the refrigerator.

Submitted by Autumn Smith

Tip: Salsa is healthy for you.

PSALM 136:1: O GIVE thanks unto the Lord; for *he* is good; for his mercy *endureth* for ever.

Think you cannot cook because you have never cooked before or are disabled? Think again!

Some recipes included are:

- Chocolate Butterscotch Pudding Cake
- Brown Sugar buttered pork chops
- Winter black bean salsa and more

Reviews for Overcoming Obstacles in Cooking

Overcoming Obstacles in Cooking is a very useful cookbook.
Writer's Digest

Overcoming Obstacles in Cooking is a rare take on instruction for the home cook.
Outskirts Press

MATTHEW W. MILLER would like this book to be used for prison ministries, suicide prevention, addiction and recovery centers, and mental hospitals.

www.ingramcontent.com/pod-product-compliance
Lightning Source LLC
Chambersburg PA
CBHW041234240426
43673CB00010B/330